The Mother's Milk

COOKBOOK

NOT JUST FOR BABIES ANYMORE

WRITTEN BY *LUX AND FRIENDS* • PHOTOGRAPHY BY *JOSHUA WALKER*

The Mother's Milk

COOKBOOK

NOT JUST FOR BABIES ANYMORE

ISBN 978-0-9965906-0-0

— DISCLAIMER —

THANK YOU FOR YOUR INTEREST IN THE MOTHER'S MILK COOKBOOK.

THE INFORMATION IN THIS BOOK IS ACCURATE, COMPLETE, AND UP TO DATE TO THE BEST OF OUR KNOWLEDGE. THE MOTHER'S MILK COOKBOOK IS INTENDED AS AN INFORMATIVE GUIDE FOR THOSE WANTING TO EXPERIENCE COOKING WITH BREAST MILK.

IT IS THE RESPONSIBILITY OF THE READER TO VERIFY IF THE PRODUCT AND RECIPE MEET YOUR PARTICULAR NEEDS. PLEASE CONSULT YOUR DOCTOR BEFORE CONSUMING BREAST MILK. IN NO WAY IS THE MOTHER'S MILK COOKBOOK INTENDED TO REPLACE OR CONFLICT WITH ANY ADVICE GIVEN BY YOUR DOCTOR OR NUTRITIONIST. THE AUTHOR AND THE PUBLISHER OF THIS BOOK RECOMMEND SCREENING THE SUPPLIER OF SAID BREAST MILK BEFORE CONSUMPTION.

THE AUTHOR AND PUBLISHER DISCLAIM ANY AND ALL LIABILITY IN CONNECTION WITH THE USE OF THE MOTHER'S MILK COOKBOOK.

IN OTHER WORDS, ENJOY BREAST MILK AT YOUR OWN RISK.

MOTHER'S CONTENTS

MAMA'S NEW ENGLAND
CLAM CHOWDER

MAKES APPROXIMATELY 6 SERVINGS

Your favorite cream-based chowder just got a lot creamier.

YOU WILL NEED :

3 cups of Mother's sweet breast milk
(Double D-Cups Work Best)

1 cup heavy cream

3 tablespoons all-purpose flour

2 cups of chicken or vegetable stock

5 teaspoons chopped bacon bits

16 ounces clams (chopped), or 18 ounces of canned
chopped baby clams

¼ cup scallions

1 cup chopped onion

1 cup chopped celery

1 teaspoon dried chopped thyme

1 lb Idaho potatoes

2 10-ounce cans of chopped clams in juice

2 bay leaves

1 teaspoon of salt

2 tablespoons unsalted butter

DIRECTIONS:

Heat the butter in a large pot over medium-high heat.

Add the onion, thyme, and celery and sauté until softened, mixing often. Stir in the flour to distribute evenly.

Add the stock, juice from 2 cans of chopped clams (reserve clams), Mama's sweet breast milk, cream, bay leaves, and potatoes and stir to combine.

Bring to a simmer, stirring consistently (the mixture will thicken), then reduce the heat to medium-low and cook 20 minutes, stirring often, until the potatoes are nice and tender.

Then add clams and season to taste with salt and pepper, cook until clams are just firm, another 2 minutes.

To serve, remove the bay leaves and divide Mama's sweet mixture into 6 bowls. Sprinkle bacon bits and scallions on top of each serving as desired.

BREAD PUDDING WITH
CHOCOLATE CHIPS

MAKES APPROXIMATELY 8 SERVINGS

One popular complaint about bread pudding is that it is constantly too dry...
... Not this one.

YOU WILL NEED :

Bread Pudding

4 cups of Mother's sweet breast milk

2 cups granulated sugar

3 lightly beaten eggs

2 ½ teaspoons vanilla

4 tablespoons unsalted butter

1 cup raisins

½ teaspoon cinnamon

¼ teaspoon allspice

1 loaf of French bread (2 to 3 days old)

½ cup of mini chocolate chips

Bourbon Sauce

½ cup melted butter

1 cup granulated sugar

1 cup bourbon

1 egg

DIRECTIONS:

Bourbon Sauce: Make the bourbon sauce by adding butter, granulated sugar, and egg to a medium saucepan. Whisk constantly over low heat until mixture thickens. Once mixture thickens, add bourbon slowly and continue to whisk. Mixture should be creamy. Remove from heat and set aside.

Bread Pudding: Cut bread into 1" squares and place in a large mixing bowl. Add breast milk and let bread soak for 1 to 2 minutes. Move bread around with fingers until all of the milk is absorbed. Set aside.

In a separate mixing bowl, add eggs, sugar, vanilla, and the remaining spices. Beat all of these ingredients together thoroughly and then gently stir in both the soaked bread and raisins.

Preheat oven to 350° F.

Spread the 4 tablespoons of unsalted butter evenly in the bottom of a 13" X 9" baking pan. Now pour in the bread mixture and bake at 350° F for approximately 40 minutes. Remove the bread pudding from the oven when the edges start getting brown.

Sprinkle the mini chocolate chips on top and serve with the bourbon sauce on the side.

MOTHER'S "PERKY" BISCUITS & SAUSAGE GRAVY

MAKES APPROXIMATELY 12 SERVINGS

This popular southern breakfast dish is about to get even more popular.

YOU WILL NEED :

Biscuits

1 cup cake flour

1 cup all-purpose flour

1 teaspoon sugar (granulated)

2 teaspoons baking powder

½ teaspoon baking soda

½ cup cold, unsalted butter (chopped
   into small squares)

¾ cup buttermilk

Sausage Gravy

4 cups of Mother's sweet breast milk

⅓ cup all-purpose flour

2 ¼ teaspoons black pepper

½ teaspoons salt

1 pound ground breakfast sausage

DIRECTIONS:

Biscuits: Preheat oven to 450° F. Set aside a large non-stick baking sheet.

In a large bowl, add sugar, baking powder, baking soda, and both of the flours. Now whisk together.

Add butter and whisk thoroughly to make sure that butter is evenly distributed throughout the mix.

Now stir in the buttermilk with a rubber spatula until the mixture becomes a sticky ball.

Place ball mixture onto a lightly floured surface and form into a round ball.

Lightly press the dough into a circle that is ¾" thick. Now use a 2" round biscuit cutter to cut out the dough into circles. Combine the remaining pieces of dough and form together into another ¾" thick circle. Use the biscuit cutter to cut out several more dough circles and discard the remaining extra dough. Place the round biscuits evenly spaced on the non-stick bake sheet.

Bake for approximately 10 minutes until the biscuits are golden brown on top. Remove biscuits and let them cool on a wire rack.

Gravy: In a large skillet, cook the ground sausage over medium-high heat until meat is no longer pink. Break apart the meat as it is cooking.

Now lower the heat to medium and add the flour slowly, stirring to dissolve it. Make sure that you add only a little flour at a time so it does not clump together as you stir it in.

After all of the flour has been dissolved, slowly pour in Mama's sweet breast milk, stirring constantly as it is added. Cook the gravy for approximately 12 minutes, stirring frequently until it starts to thicken. Add the salt and pepper and cook until gravy becomes the desired thickness.

Pour Mama's sweet gravy over the biscuits and serve.

15

MAMA'S MARVELOUS
VANILLA BEAN SHAKE

MAKES APPROXIMATELY 2 SERVINGS

Will leave you with a milk mustache you can be proud of.

YOU WILL NEED :

1 cup of Mother's sweet breast milk

2 cups of crushed ice

⅓ cup of vanilla flavored syrup

4 tablespoons of whipped cream

1 scoop of vanilla ice cream

DIRECTIONS:

Chop ice in blender.

Add breast milk.

Add 1 scoop of vanilla ice cream.

Add vanilla syrup.

Blend mixture until smooth.

Pour mixture into 2 glasses.

Add 2 tablespoons of whipped cream on top of each glass.

Serve immediately.

SHEPHERD'S PIE

MAKES APPROXIMATELY 8 SERVINGS

Whether you call it a Shepherds Pie or the more traditional Cottage Pie, one thing is certain, you have never had one like this before.

YOU WILL NEED:

1 cup of Mother's sweet breast milk

2 ½ pounds of russet potatoes, peeled

¼ cup all-purpose flour

1 ½ teaspoon salt

1 teaspoon coarse ground black pepper

1 tablespoon vegetable or canola oil

1 teaspoon dried thyme

1 ¼ cup yellow shredded sharp cheddar cheese

1 cup chopped onion

1 cup frozen peas

1 cup chopped celery

1 cup chopped carrots

½ cup tomato paste

2 pounds ground beef

1 cup water

DIRECTIONS:

Place potatoes in a large saucepan. Fill pan with water until potatoes are completely covered in water and add a pinch of salt to the water. Potatoes should be approximately 1-inch below the water level. Bring water to a boil and then reduce the heat, and let the potatoes simmer for about 18 minutes. Potatoes should be soft enough to easily pierce with a fork. Set potatoes aside.

Preheat oven to 450° F.

Heat oil in a 6 quart stockpot over medium to high heat. Add thyme, carrots, celery, and onion. Cook stirring 8 to 10 minutes until vegetables are tender. Add tomato paste and flour while stirring. Add ground beef stirring occasionally until beef is browned. This should take approximately 8 minutes. Once meat is brown, add peas and 1 cup of water and bring to a boil. Reduce heat and simmer for 2 minutes, stirring mixture. Turn off heat and set mixture aside.

Now take and drain the water from the potatoes, but keep the potatoes in the pan. Cook over medium heat for 1 to 2 minutes until any excess water has evaporated from the pan. Remove from heat and add Mama's sweet breast milk and 1 cup of the shredded cheddar cheese. Add salt and pepper and mash until smooth.

Pour beef mixture into a 13" X 9" baking dish. Spread evenly with a spatula. Now spoon mashed potato mixture on top using the back of the spoon to spread evenly. Sprinkle remaining cheddar cheese on top of potato mixture and bake uncovered for approximately 20 to 25 minutes. Remove once topping has browned slightly. Let stand for 3 to 5 minutes before serving.

MOTHER'S SWEET &
CREAMY COLESLAW

MAKES APPROXIMATELY 8 SERVINGS

Usually a boring side dish, not anymore.

YOU WILL NEED :

¼ cup of Mother's sweet breast milk

½ cup of mayonnaise

¼ cup of buttermilk

½ cup granulated sugar

½ teaspoon of salt

¼ teaspoon of ground black pepper

1 ½ teaspoons distilled white vinegar

2 ½ teaspoons fresh lemon juice

8 cups finely chopped cabbage (fresh)

⅓ cup fresh grated carrots

DIRECTIONS:

Whisk together sugar, salt, pepper, breast milk, mayonnaise, buttermilk, lemon juice and white vinegar. Keep whisking until smooth.

Add chopped cabbage and grated carrots. Mix until blended thoroughly with dressing.

Refrigerate for at least 2 to 3 hours before serving.

STACKED SOUTHERN FRIED CHICKEN

MAKES APPROXIMATELY 4 SERVINGS

The skin is the best part of any fried chicken. Well guess what folks, the best part just got better.

YOU WILL NEED :

1 cup of Mother's sweet breast milk
(Double D-Cups work best)

1 whole chicken (cut up into frying pieces)

2 large eggs

1 ½ cups self-rising flour

3 ½ cups peanut oil

1 teaspoon ground black pepper

1 ½ tablespoons of salt

DIRECTIONS:

In a medium bowl, beat the large eggs and stir in the sweet breast milk. Then add the salt and pepper and mix lightly.

Place the chicken pieces in the breast milk mixture and let them soak for 10 minutes turning chicken over once half way through.

Thoroughly roll chicken pieces in flour making sure to coat each piece completely. Then set chicken aside to dry.

Heat peanut oil in a large cast-iron skillet to 350° F. Now add the thighs and legs to the hot oil. After 3 to 4 minutes, add the breast pieces to the oil making sure not to overcrowd the skillet.

Let chicken cook until chicken is brown on one side (about 5 minutes). Turn chicken over and brown the other side (about 5 minutes). Reduce heat to medium low and cook chicken covered for 15 minutes. Turn chicken over and cook covered for another 10 minutes. Remove cover and cook for an additional 5 minutes.

Remove chicken from skillet and place on a serving dish allowing chicken to rest for 1 to 2 minutes. Chicken should be crisp and ready to serve.

BUSTY
WHITE RUSSIAN

MAKES APPROXIMATELY 1 SERVING

The only thing better than a White Russian; A busty white Russian.

YOU WILL NEED :

½ cup of Mother's sweet breast milk
(Freshly pumped)

3 ounces heavy cream

1 ½ ounce of vodka

½ ounce of coffee flavored liqueur

DIRECTIONS:

In a mixing glass combine
breast milk, Half & Half milk,
vodka and coffee flavored
liqueur.

Pour over ice and serve
in a tall glass.

MOTHER'S MILK-BRAISED PORK CHOPS

MAKES APPROXIMATELY 4 SERVINGS

Classy enough for fine dining, cozy enough for a family barbecue.

YOU WILL NEED :

2 cups of Mother's sweet breast milk, divided

4 pork loin chops (1 inch thick, each)

1 teaspoon margarine

½ teaspoon of salt

½ teaspoons of ground black pepper

2 tablespoons all-purpose flour

DIRECTIONS:

Trim fat from chops. Combine flour, salt, and pepper in a large zip-lock plastic bag. Dip chops in breast milk. Add chops to the mixture; seal bag, and shake to coat chops with flour mixture. Remove chops from bag, reserving the remaining flour mixture. Place the flour mixture in a small bowl. Gradually add 1 cup milk, stirring with a wire whisk until blended.

Melt margarine in a large skillet over medium-high heat. Add chops; cook 3 minutes on each side or until browned. Add milk mixture; cover, reduce heat to low, and cook 30 minutes, stirring occasionally.

Turn the chops over. Add remaining 1 cup milk; cover and cook 30 minutes, stirring occasionally.

Uncover skillet, and cook the chops an additional 15 minutes or until the liquid is reduced to ¼ cup (the sauce will be very thick). Spoon sauce over chops.

CHICKEN FRIED STEAK WITH
CREAMY WHITE GRAVY

MAKES APPROXIMATELY 4 SERVINGS

*Another classic southern dish, a perfect pairing with
Mother's Mashed Potatoes and Gravy.*

YOU WILL NEED :

Chicken Fried Steak

2 cups of Mother's sweet breast milk

1 ½ pounds of cube steak cut into small hamburger-sized
  steaks

½ cups canola oil

2 cups of all-purpose flour

2 teaspoons salt

3 teaspoons freshly ground black pepper

2 teaspoons of seasoning salt

2 large eggs

Creamy White Gravy

2 cups of Mother's sweet breast milk

1 teaspoon of freshly ground black pepper

1 teaspoon salt

⅓ cup all-purpose flour

2 tablespoons butter

DIRECTIONS:

Chicken Fried Steak: Gently pound cube steaks wrapped in wax paper with a meat tenderizer. Season steaks with salt and 2 teaspoons pepper and set aside. Preheat oven to 275° F.

In a medium size bowl, whisk together breast milk and eggs. In a large bowl, mix together flour, seasoning salt, and one teaspoon of pepper.

Heat canola oil in a large skillet over medium-high heat.

Dredge cube steaks in flour mixture. Take cube steaks directly from the flour mixture and dip each steak into the milk and egg mixture. Now return each steak back into the flour mixture for a final coating. Set coated steaks aside.

Cook coated cube steaks in the warm oil until golden brown (approximately 3 ½ minutes on each side). Place cooked cube steaks on a baking sheet in oven to keep warm. Save 2 tablespoons of the oil from the skillet to use with the gravy.

Gravy: Warm the 2 tablespoons of canola you saved in a medium sauté pan over medium-high heat. Whisk in flour, freshly ground black pepper, and salt to create a roux. Now whisk in the 2 cups of breast milk and butter making a gravy. Bring gravy to a boil. Reduce heat to low and cook thickening to desired consistency (approximately 10 minutes).

Remove warm chicken fried steaks from oven. Spoon warm creamy white gravy over chicken fried steaks and serve.

CREAM NIPPED
BEEF ON TOAST

MAKES APPROXIMATELY 2 SERVINGS

A perfect first course that will leave you wanting more.

YOU WILL NEED :

1 ½ cups of Mother's sweet breast milk

4 tablespoons butter

3 tablespoons all-purpose flour

¼ teaspoon cayenne pepper

1 jar of dried sliced beef (8 ounce)

4 slices of thick white sandwich bread

DIRECTIONS:

Melt butter in a medium saucepan over low heat and then whisk in flour quickly to form a roux.

Whisk in breast milk very slowly and increase heat to medium high. Cook, stirring until thickened.

Once mixture has thickened, add sliced beef and cayenne pepper and bring to a boil. Stir as needed.

Toast slices of white bread to a golden brown. Place 2 slices of finished toast on separate plates and spoon hot creamy beef mixture evenly over toast. Serve immediately.

NACHOS WITH CREAMY CHEESE SAUCE & JALAPEÑOS

MAKES APPROXIMATELY 4 SERVINGS

The jalapeños give this dish a perfect kick, and the creamy cheese sauce will bring you back down. These nachos are like a roller coaster for your mouth.

YOU WILL NEED :

1 cup of Mother's sweet breast milk

½ teaspoon salt

2 tablepoons all-purpose flour

2 tablespoons butter

7 slices processed American cheese

1 bag of tortilla chips (approximately 12 ounces)

½ cup jalapeño pepper slices (store bought in the jar)

DIRECTIONS:

Melt butter in a medium saucepan over medium heat and whisk in all-purpose flour. Add in breast milk and stir until the mixture thickens.

Now add in cheese and salt stirring continuously. Stir and cook until cheese has melted and all of the ingredients are thoroughly mixed. This should take approximately 12 minutes.

Divide tortilla chips into 4 bowls. Pour hot creamy cheese mixture over tortilla chips and top with jalapeño pepper slices as desired. Serve immediately while cheese is hot.

HOT MOTHER'S CREAMY GRITS

MAKES APPROXIMATELY 4 SERVINGS

Traditionally grits are served as a breakfast side dish, but these grits have enough calcium in them to give your morning the boost you are looking for.

YOU WILL NEED :

*4 cups of Mother's sweet breast milk
(Double D-Cups Work Best)*

4 cups water

2 cups white stone-ground grits

½ cup heavy cream

½ stick unsalted butter (optional), cut into pieces

2 teaspoons kosher salt

DIRECTIONS:

Bring water and milk just to a simmer in a 4- to 5-quart heavy saucepan. Meanwhile, cover grits with water in a large bowl and whisk vigorously. Let stand 30 seconds, then skim any chaff that has floated to surface with a fine-mesh sieve. Drain grits well in a fine-mesh sieve and whisk into simmering milk mixture.

Reduce heat to low and simmer grits, partially covered, stirring often with a heatproof rubber spatula, until grits are tender and thickened to the consistency of loose oatmeal, about 1 ¼ hours (stir more toward end of cooking to avoid scorching). If grits become too thick before they are tender and creamy, thin with hot water (about ½ cup).

Stir in cream, butter (if using), and salt. Remove from heat and keep warm, covered, up to 20 minutes.

MASCARPONE "NATURALLY" STUFFED CREPES

MAKES APPROXIMATELY 6 SERVINGS

Let's give the French a round of applause for this breakfast favorite, you can give Mothers Milk a round of applause for improving upon it.

YOU WILL NEED :

Crepes

1 cup of Mother's sweet breast milk

3 large eggs

¼ cup water

1 cup all-purpose flour

¼ cup unsalted butter (melted)

3 teaspoons sugar

1 teaspoon pure vanilla extract

1 small pinch of salt

Filling

1 ½ cups low fat cream cheese

1 ½ cups mascarpone

½ cup sugar

½ teaspoon pure vanilla extract

½ cup freshly squeezed orange juice

1 ½ tablespoons finely grated orange zest

DIRECTIONS:

Crepes: In a blender or food processor, blend the flour, sugar, and salt. Then add the breast milk, water, eggs, butter, and vanilla extract and blend until mixture is smooth. Set crepe mixture aside in refrigerator for 45 minutes.

Filling: Whisk the mascarpone, cream cheese, sugar, orange zest, orange juice, and vanilla extract in a small mixing bowl. Set aside.

Once crepe batter has been refrigerated for 45 minutes, heat a 6-inch nonstick skillet over medium heat. The skillet will be at the correct temperature when a drop of water bounces and then evaporates when dropped in the center of skillet. Now pour about ¼ cup of crepe batter into the skillet coating the bottom of the skillet evenly. Cook crepe batter for about 30 seconds until batter sets and then carefully flip the crepe over. Cook the crepe just long enough on this side for the bottom to just start to turn golden brown and then remove the crepe from the pan. Repeat these steps, cooking the rest of the crepe batter. Stack the finished crepes with a piece of wax paper between each crepe as they finish cooking.

Now spoon the cheese filling into the center of each crepe and roll crepe around filling, resembling a burrito, but leaving the ends open. Divide the filling evenly among the cooked crepes. Serve as is, or with berries of choice on top.

HOMEMADE STRAWBERRY YOGURT WITH GRANOLA

MAKES APPROXIMATELY 2 SERVINGS

Give your taste buds a workout with this breakfast favorite.

YOU WILL NEED :

¼ cup of Mother's sweet breast milk

¾ cup of water

1 pound of frozen strawberries

1 cup sugar

1 pint plain yogurt

½ cup of your favorite granola

DIRECTIONS:

Combine water and breast milk in a medium saucepan over medium heat and then dissolve sugar in water and milk mixture.

Add in frozen strawberries and bring to a low boil. Keep at a low boil for 10 minutes stirring occasionally.

After 10 minutes, remove strawberries from heat and pour mixture through a strainer over a bowl, removing strawberries and saving syrup.

Mix ¼ cup of syrup with 1 pint of plain yogurt in a mixer at a low to medium speed. Taste and add more syrup if it is not sweet enough for your liking. Place mixed yogurt in refrigerator overnight to allow it to set.

Serve in a small bowl or glass. Sprinkle granola over top as desired.

MOTHER'S "BEEF STROKEN-OFF"

MAKES APPROXIMATELY 4 SERVINGS

The Russians created this amazing dish in the 19ᵗʰ century, but perhaps they were missing one key ingredient.

YOU WILL NEED :

½ cup of Mother's sweet breast milk

1 pound top sirloin strips (cut 2 inch long by ½ inch wide)

½ cup of sour cream

¼ cup of heavy cream

½ cup of beef broth

1 medium onion (chopped thinly)

4 teaspoons of butter

1 teaspoon yellow mustard

1 teaspoon salt

1 teaspoon fresh ground black pepper

8 ounces of medium egg noodles (cooked)

6 ounces of fresh mushrooms

2 tablespoons of all-purpose flour

DIRECTIONS:

Sear top sirloin strips on both sides in a large nonstick skillet (30 seconds on each side). Remove seared meat from skillet and set aside. Save meat juice.

In a small mixing bowl, mix together breast milk, sour cream, heavy cream, beef broth, and mustard. Set aside.

Clean skillet and melt butter at medium low heat. Add in chopped onions. Sauté until golden brown (about 7-10 minutes).

Now lower heat and stir in flour for about 60 seconds. Add in milk and cream mixture while whisking. Add leftover meat juice and simmer for about 7 minutes until mushroom sauce thickens. Now add seared top sirloin strips to sauce and season with salt and pepper. Heat and stir occasionally until meat is warmed through.

Spoon meat mixture warm over egg noodles and sprinkle parsley over top and serve.

CREAMY
MACARONI & CHEESE

MAKES APPROXIMATELY 6 SERVINGS

Just when you thought mac & cheese couldn't possibly get any better.

YOU WILL NEED :

1 ½ cups of Mother's sweet breast milk

2 cups elbow macaroni (uncooked)

½ cup of butter (cubed)

½ cup of prepared cheese such as Velveeta (cubed)

2 cups of cheddar cheese (shredded)

⅓ cup of freshly grated Parmesan cheese

½ cup all-purposed flour

1 cup of sour cream

½ teaspoon of ground mustard

1 teaspoon of salt

DIRECTIONS:

Preheat oven to 350° F. In a medium to large pot, cook the elbow macaroni by following the directions located on the package. Once pasta is cooked, drain macaroni and toss with cheddar cheese in a large mixing bowl. Set aside.

Melt cubed butter in a large saucepan and stir in all-purpose flour until mixture is smooth. Add breast milk slowly and bring to a boil. Lower heat to medium and cook, stirring continuously until mixture has thickened (approximately 3 minutes). Now add prepared cheese, sour cream, Parmesan cheese, salt and mustard. Stir until cheese is melted and cream sauce is smooth.

Take finished cream sauce and mix with macaroni cheddar mixture. Stir until evenly mixed.

Spread combined mixture evenly into a 3 quart greased baking dish. Bake uncovered at 350° F until golden brown and cheese is bubbly (approximately 35 minutes). Serve immediately while hot.

CREAMY "HOTTIE" COCOA

MAKES APPROXIMATELY 4 SERVINGS

Be sure not to burn your tongue on this hottie.

YOU WILL NEED :

2 cups of Mother's sweet breast milk

4 ½ cups of hot water

1 can of sweetened condensed milk (14 ounces)

½ cup of unsweetened cocoa

1 teaspoon of vanilla extract

1 small pinch of salt

Whipped cream topping or 1 cup of mini marshmallows (optional)

DIRECTIONS:

In a large saucepan combine condensed milk, vanilla extract, unsweetened cocoa and salt. Place saucepan over medium heat and slowly stir in breast milk and hot water. Heat stirring until temperature is warm to hot (do not bring to a boil).

Divide "Hottie" Cocoa into 4 mugs and serve topped with whipped cream or mini marshmallows as desired.

HOMEMADE VANILLA YOGURT WITH GRANOLA

MAKES APPROXIMATELY 4 SERVINGS

There is nothing plain about this vanilla yogurt.

YOU WILL NEED :

1 cup of Mother's sweet breast milk

½ teaspoon of pure vanilla extract

1 teaspoon brown sugar

2 teaspoons of honey

1 small pinch of ground cinnamon

1 pint plain yogurt

½ cup of your favorite granola or berries

DIRECTIONS:

Heat breast milk in a small saucepan over medium heat. Add brown sugar and cinnamon and stir until brown sugar dissolves.

Stir in honey and pure vanilla extract. Keep stirring until well blended.

Once blended, remove from heat.

Mix ¼ cup of honey milk mixture with 1 pint of plain yogurt in a mixer at a low to medium speed. Taste and add more syrup if more vanilla taste is desired. Place mixed yogurt in refrigerator overnight to allow it to set.

Serve in a small bowl or glass. Sprinkle ½ cup of your favorite granola or berries over top as desired.

HOMEMADE BLUEBERRY YOGURT WITH GRANOLA

MAKES APPROXIMATELY 2 SERVINGS

How can something that tastes this good be so good for you?

YOU WILL NEED :

¼ cup of Mother's sweet breast milk

¾ cup of water

1 pound of frozen blueberries

1 cup sugar

1 pint plain yogurt

½ cup of your favorite granola

DIRECTIONS:

Combine water and breast milk in a medium saucepan over medium heat and then dissolve sugar in water and milk mixture.

Add in frozen blueberries and bring to a low boil. Keep at low boil for 10 minutes stirring occasionally.

After 10 minutes, remove blueberries from heat and pour mixture through a strainer over a bowl removing blueberries and saving syrup.

Mix ¼ cup of syrup with 1 pint of plain yogurt in a mixer at a low to medium speed. Taste to test and add more syrup if it is not sweet enough for your liking. Place mixed yogurt in refrigerator overnight to allow it to set.

Serve in a small bowl or glass. Sprinkle granola over top as desired. You can also place a few fresh blueberries on top if you have them available.

HOMEMADE PEACH YOGURT WITH GRANOLA

MAKES APPROXIMATELY 2 SERVINGS

Peachy, breast milky, breakfast goodness.

YOU WILL NEED :

¼ cup of Mother's sweet breast milk

¾ cup of water

1 pound of frozen peach slices

1 cup sugar

1 pint plain yogurt

½ cup of your favorite granola

DIRECTIONS:

Combine water and breast milk in a medium saucepan over medium heat and then dissolve sugar in water and milk mixture.

Add in frozen peaches and bring to a low boil. Keep at a low boil for 10 minutes stirring occasionally.

After 10 minutes, remove peaches from heat and pour mixture through a strainer over a bowl removing peaches and saving syrup.

Mix ¼ cup of syrup with 1 pint of plain yogurt in a mixer at a low to medium speed. Taste to test and add more syrup if it is not sweet enough for your liking. Place mixed yogurt in refrigerator overnight to allow it to set.

Serve in a small bowl or glass. Sprinkle granola over top as desired. Add a fresh peach slice on top for garnish if you have it available

MOTHER'S STRAWBERRY HOTCAKES

MAKES APPROXIMATELY 6 SERVINGS

They say breakfast is the most important meal of the day, and you can't go wrong with this amazing recipe.

YOU WILL NEED :

1 cup of Mother's sweet breast milk

1 extra large egg

½ cup of butter (cubed)

2 ¼ cups fresh strawberries (washed and sliced)

1 ¼ cups all-purpose flour

2 tablespoons of baking powder

2 ½ teaspoons granulated sugar

½ teaspoon of pure vanilla extract

½ tablespoon of salt

Syrup for serving

DIRECTIONS:

Set aside 2 medium mixing bowls. Preheat a nonstick griddle over medium heat. Melt one tablespoon of the cubed butter in the microwave and set aside.

In one bowl, whisk together granulated sugar, all-purpose flour, baking powder and salt. In the other bowl, whisk together breast milk, egg and vanilla extract. Now slowly add the breast milk mixture into the flour mixture continuously whisking. Stir in the melted butter and whisk until the batter is thick and smooth. Now fold in the sliced strawberries into the batter.

Cook the pancakes by spooning ¼ cup of the batter onto the griddle. Flip pancakes over with a spatula once batter becomes set and thoroughly bubbly (approximately 3 minutes). Cook on other side until pancakes are golden brown and remove from heat (approximately 2 minutes). Repeat process until all of the batter is used.

Serve with butter and syrup. You can also top with fresh strawberry slices if desired.

MOTHER'S MASHED POTATOES & GRAVY

MAKES APPROXIMATELY 4 SERVINGS

A couple mounds of these mashed potatoes are the perfect compliment to any number of main courses.

YOU WILL NEED :

Mashed Potatoes

¼ cup of Mother's sweet breast milk

1 ½ pounds of Yukon Gold potatoes
(peeled and cut into wedges)

¼ cup heavy cream

2 ½ teaspoons butter

1 ½ teaspoons of kosher salt

1 teaspoon ground black pepper

Country Gravy

1 tablespoon of Mother's sweet breast milk

¼ pound unsalted butter

2 yellow onions, chopped

1 teaspoon kosher salt

¼ cup all-purpose flour

½ teaspoon ground black pepper

2 cups chicken stock, heated

1 tablespoon cognac or 1 tablespoon brandy

DIRECTIONS:

Mashed Potatoes: Place potatoes in a medium saucepan. Pour in enough water to cover potatoes and add ½ teaspoon of salt. Turn on heat and bring to a boil. Once water has reached a boil, reduce heat and simmer covered for 20 minutes. Potatoes should be soft enough to easily cut with a fork. Set aside.

In a small saucepan, melt butter and warm heavy cream over low heat.

Remove potatoes from water and place in a medium size mixing bowl. Mash potatoes with a potato masher or with the a fork. Stir in heavy cream and butter mixture. Once potatoes are mashed and mixed with heavy cream mixture, mix in breast milk stirring until desired consistency is reached. Add salt and pepper to taste. Set mashed potatoes aside.

Country Gravy: In a large sauté pan, cook the butter and onions on medium-low heat for 12 to 15 minutes, until the onions are lightly browned.

Sprinkle the flour into the pan, whisk in, then add the salt and pepper. Cook for 2 to 3 minutes. Add the hot chicken stock and cognac, and cook uncovered for 4 to 5 minutes until thickened. Add Mama's sweet breast milk and serve.

MOTHER'S
CREAMED SPINACH

MAKES APPROXIMATELY 4 SERVINGS

If this isn't the creamiest spinach you have ever had,
you are probably doing it wrong.

YOU WILL NEED :

¼ cup of Mother's sweet breast milk

½ cup of heavy cream

2 pounds of fresh baby spinach

2 tablespoons butter (unsalted)

1 tablespoon olive oil

1 whole onion (minced)

1 teaspoon fresh minced garlic

Salt and pepper to taste

DIRECTIONS:

Wash and remove stems from spinach.

Place a large pot over medium heat. Add olive oil and unsalted butter stirring until the butter melts. Add minced onion and garlic to the pot, allowing them to cook for about 5 minutes until both are soft. Now add spinach to the pot slowly, one handful at a time. Make sure that spinach begins to wilt before adding the next handful. Repeat this step until all of the spinach is in the pot.

Continue to cook, stirring occasionally until the spinach is dry. Once spinach becomes dry, lower the heat and add the breast milk and heavy cream. Continue to cook for 10 additional minutes stirring occasionally.

Remove creamed spinach from heat and serve with salt and pepper to taste.

MOTHER'S EASY PUMPKIN PIE

MAKES APPROXIMATELY 8 SERVINGS

"Bust" this pie out for Thanksgiving and your guests will have plenty to be thankful for.

YOU WILL NEED :

¼ cup of Mother's sweet breast milk

1 can sweetened condensed milk (14 ounces)

2 large eggs

1 can pumpkin puree (16 ounce)

2 teaspoons butter (unsalted)

1 unbaked pie crust (9 inch)

1 tablespoon pumpkin pie spice

1 teaspoon vanilla extract

DIRECTIONS:

In a large size bowl, mix together Mama's sweet breast milk, sweetened condensed milk, large eggs, pumpkin puree, pumpkin pie spice, and vanilla extract. Mix together until well combined.

Preheat oven to 425° F.

Place pie crust into a 9 inch pie dish pressing down on dough to fit pie crust to dish. Pour pumpkin puree mixture into pie crust evenly. Melt the 2 teaspoons of butter in the microwave and brush butter lightly on the outer edge of the pie crust.

Place pie on a baking pan and bake pie in oven at 425° F for 15 minutes. Now reduce heat to 350° F and bake until filling sets (approximately 35 minutes). Remove from oven.

Let pie cool for at least 30 minutes on counter and then refrigerate. Serve chilled.

"MOTOR BOATIN" BLUEBERRY MUFFINS

MAKES APPROXIMATELY 12 SERVINGS

As if motor boating wasn't fun enough, try these muffins on for size.

YOU WILL NEED :

¼ cup of Mother's sweet breast milk

¼ cup of whole milk (from the cow)

2 ½ cups of fresh blueberries (washed)

2 large eggs

1 stick unsalted butter (softened)

2 cups all-purpose flour

1 ¼ cups granulated sugar

2 teaspoons baking powder

¼ teaspoon ground cinnamon

1 teaspoon pure vanilla extract

½ teaspoon of salt

DIRECTIONS:

In a small bowl, mash ¾ cup of the blueberries with the back of a fork. Set aside.

In a medium bowl, whisk the butter until it becomes creamy and smooth. Transfer the creamed butter to an electric mixer. Add 1 cup of granulated sugar and mix slowly. Now add the large eggs, vanilla extract, baking powder, cinnamon, and salt and keep the mixer mixing at slow speed. Now add the mashed blueberries and mix again.

Line a muffin tin with paper liners and preheat oven to 375° F.

Set the mixer on low speed and add 1 cup of the flour and the cow's milk. As soon as the batter is well mixed, add the remaining flour and Mama's sweet breast milk. Continue to mix at slow speed until well mixed. Remove bowl from mixer and fold in the remaining blueberries by hand using a small spatula.

Use a large spoon to fill the muffin cups ¾ of the way up. Mix together the remaining sugar with the cinnamon and sprinkle on the top of each muffin. Place muffin pan in the oven and bake until batter has risen and is golden brown (approximately 25 minutes). Remove pan from oven and let cool for at least 30 minutes. Remove muffins from pan and serve.

MOTHER'S "EASY" LASAGNA

MAKES APPROXIMATELY 9 SERVINGS

This classic Italian favorite is perfect for the whole family.

YOU WILL NEED :

½ cup of Mother's sweet breast milk

1 pound ground beef

12 lasagna noodles (cooked and drained)

1 large egg

1 jar of your favorite marinara pasta sauce (24 ounces)

15 ounces of part-skim ricotta cheese

2 cups shredded mozzarella cheese

1 cup shredded cheddar cheese

½ cup grated Parmesan cheese

DIRECTIONS:

In a medium skillet, brown ground beef and drain fat. Lower heat and stir in your favorite pasta sauce. Cook stirring occasionally until warm throughout.

Preheat oven to 375° F.

In a large bowl combine mozzarella cheese, ricotta cheese, Parmesan cheese, breast milk and egg. Stir until well mixed. Set aside.

In a 13" X 9" baking dish, spread 1 cup of the meat sauce evenly on the bottom. Then layer 4 lasagna noodles on top, covering the meat sauce. Add another cup of the meat sauce to the top of the noodles and spread evenly. Next, spoon on ½ of the cheese and breast milk mixture. Cover again with 4 lasagna noodles. Repeat with the meat sauce and milk cheese mixture one more time, and cover again with the last 4 noodles. Top noodles with remaining sauce and sprinkle the cup of shredded cheddar cheese evenly on top. Cover dish with aluminum foil and bake in oven for 30 minutes. Remove foil and bake uncovered for another 5 minutes.

Remove lasagna from oven and let stand 10 minutes. Slice lasagna with a knife into 9 squares and serve.

MOTHER'S
SIMPLE CHEESECAKE

—————— MAKES APPROXIMATELY 12 SERVINGS ——————

We have heard of strawberry cheesecake, tiramisu cheesecake, pumpkin cheesecake, etc.
...But make room for the mother of them all.

YOU WILL NEED :

Filling

1/4 cup of Mother's sweet breast milk

1 cup granulated sugar

3 large eggs

2 tablespoons all-purpose flour

3 packages softened cream cheese (8 ounces each)

1 tablespoon pure vanilla extract

Crust

1 3/4 cups of graham cracker crumbs

1 tablespoon *granulated sugar*

1/2 cup butter (melted)

DIRECTIONS:

Filling: Use an electric mixer to beat the cream cheese, breast milk, flour, vanilla extract and the cup of granulated sugar until blended. Turn mixer speed to low and add 1 egg at a time, mixing until all 3 eggs are blended. Set filling aside.

Crust: Preheat oven to 325° F.

In a medium size bowl mix graham cracker crumbs, melted butter and the 1 tablespoon of granulated sugar. Then press the graham cracker mix into the bottom of a 9 inch spring form pan.

Pour cream cheese filling into pie crust. Bake cheesecake in oven until center of filling is almost set (approximately 30-45 minutes). Remove cheesecake from oven and loosen the edge of the cake from the rim of the pan. Allow cheesecake to cool before removing rim from pan.

Refrigerate for at least 4 hours. Cut cheesecake into 12 even slices and serve.

MOTHER'S SWEET
OATMEAL COOKIES

—— MAKES APPROXIMATELY 12 SERVINGS ——

These sweet oatmeal cookies will melt in your mouth.

YOU WILL NEED :

¼ cup of Mother's sweet breast milk

2 large eggs

3 cups of oatmeal, uncooked

1 cup of raisins

1 cup brown sugar

1 cup white sugar

2 cups all-purpose flour

1 teaspoon baking soda

1½ teaspoons ground cinnamon

1 teaspoon vanilla extract

1 cup butter, softened

1 teaspoon salt

DIRECTIONS:

Preheat oven to 375° F.

In a medium bowl, add Mama's sweet breast milk, eggs (beat in one at a time), raisins, and vanilla. Cream together butter and sugars in a separate bowl.

Combine flour, salt, cinnamon, and baking soda. Stir into the creamed mixture. Blend in the egg-raisin mixture, and then mix in the oats. Dough will be stiff. Cover and chill dough for one hour.

Drop by heaping tablespoons onto a greased cookie sheet, or roll into balls and flatten slightly.

Bake at 375° F for 8-10 minutes or until lightly browned.

Server oatmeal cookies warm or cold as desired. Cookies go well with a cold glass of cow's milk, but don't let Mama see you drink it.

MOTHER'S CHOCOLATE CREAM PIE

MAKES APPROXIMATELY 6 SERVINGS

Chocolate + cream + pie + breast milk = OMG.

YOU WILL NEED :

1 ½ cups of Mother's sweet breast milk

1 ½ cups whole milk (from the cow)

3 egg yolks (beaten)

1 nine inch pie crust (baked)

½ cup cocoa powder (unsweetened)

1 tablespoon butter

1 cup granulated sugar

3 tablespoons cornstarch

1 ½ teaspoons pure vanilla extract

½ teaspoon salt

8 ounce container frozen whipped topping (thawed)

1 milk chocolate candy bar

DIRECTIONS:

In a large mixing bowl, blend together the granulated sugar and egg yolks. Then mix in cocoa powder, cornstarch, and salt. Now slowly stir in Mama's sweet breast milk and cow's milk.

Transfer mixture into a large saucepan and cook over medium heat, stirring continuously. Keep stirring until mixture comes to a boil. Remove from heat and stir in butter and pure vanilla extract. Allow mixture to cool for approximately 10 minutes.

Pour cool mixture into cooked pie crust and refrigerate. Once filling has chilled and set, spread thawed whipped topping evenly on top of pie. Use a cheese grater or sharp knife to shave ½ of chocolate candy bar. Sprinkle chocolate shavings on top of whipped topping as desired. Cut cream pie into 6 slices and serve.

MOTHER'S
CHEESY CHICKEN PASTA

MAKES APPROXIMATELY 6 SERVINGS

This rich and creamy dish is a winner for kids and adults alike.

YOU WILL NEED :

1 ½ cups of Mother's sweet breast milk

1 ½ cups low-fat milk (from the cow)

½ cup of white wine (dry)

8 ounces penne pasta

3 cups shredded chicken (cooked)

1 ½ cups Swiss cheese (shredded)

1 cup cauliflower florets (half inch)

1 cup broccoli florets (half inch)

½ cup finely chopped onion (fresh)

1 ½ teaspoons extra-virgin olive oil

1 teaspoon Dijon mustard

3 tablespoons all-purpose flour

1 teaspoon salt

¾ teaspoon ground black pepper

2 tablespoons fresh chives (chopped)

DIRECTIONS:

Fill a large pot halfway up with water and bring to a boil. Add penne pasta and cook for 5 minutes. Now add broccoli and cauliflower florets and continue cooking until florets and pasta are both tender (approximately 5 minutes). Using a colander, drain and rinse pasta and florets and transfer back to the pot.

In a large saucepan, heat olive oil over medium heat. Add chopped onion to pan and cook, stirring until tender (approximately 3 minutes). Add white wine and cook for 1 ½ minutes until reduced slightly.

In a medium bowl, whisk in breast milk, cow's milk, all-purpose flour, salt, and pepper. Now add this milk mixture to the pan with the chopped onions and bring to a boil over medium-high heat while stirring continuously. Cook until mixture thickens (approximately 2 minutes). Reduce heat to low and stir in Swiss cheese until smooth. Mix in chicken and mustard to cheese sauce and cook until warmed through (approximately 3 minutes).

Add the finished cheese sauce to the drained pasta and florets. Serve cheesy chicken pasta warm and garnish by sprinkling chives on top as desired.

MOTHER'S RICH CHOCOLATE SHAKE

MAKES APPROXIMATELY 2 SERVINGS

If this Mother's Milk recipe is not one of your favorites, you should get your damn taste buds checked.

YOU WILL NEED :

½ cup of Mother's sweet breast milk

½ cup of whole milk (from the cow)

2 cups of your favorite chocolate ice cream

½ cup of chocolate syrup

Whipped cream (optional)

DIRECTIONS:

In an electric blender, add all of the ingredients and process until smooth.

Pour ice cream mixture into two chilled glasses and serve immediately. Top chocolate shakes with whipped topping if desired.

MOTHER'S CORNBREAD

MAKES APPROXIMATELY 12 SERVINGS

This classic dessert dish is so good, you will want to enjoy it as a first course.

YOU WILL NEED :

½ cup of Mother's sweet breast milk

½ cup of whole milk (from the cow)

1 cup all-purpose flour

1 ¼ cup yellow cornmeal

½ cup granulated sugar

¼ cup butter, melted

1 large egg

1 tablespoon baking powder

½ teaspoon salt

DIRECTIONS:

Preheat oven to 400° F.

In a large bowl, mix together cornmeal, all-purpose flour, granulated sugar, baking powder and salt. Add in large egg, breast milk, cow's milk and butter. Stir together until batter is well combined.

Pour batter into a 9 inch round or square pan that has been greased. Place pan on center oven rack and bake for approximately 20 to 25 minutes. Test for doneness by inserting a toothpick into the center of loaf and pulling it out. Toothpick should come out clean.

With a knife, cut cornbread into squares or slices and serve.

MOTHER'S MOZZARELLA STICKS

MAKES APPROXIMATELY 6 SERVINGS

Bet you can't have just one.

YOU WILL NEED :

1 package of 12 ounce mozzarella string cheese

½ cup of Mother's sweet breast milk

2 eggs

¼ cup all-purpose flour

1 cup of Italian-style bread crumbs

Optional cup of warmed marinara sauce for dipping

DIRECTIONS:

Preheat oven to 400°F. Place flour in a shallow dish. Beat egg and milk in a separate shallow dish. Empty Italian bread crumbs into a third shallow dish.

Coat cheese sticks in flour, then dip in egg mixture. Coat evenly with bread crumbs. Discard any remaining flour, egg mixture and bread crumbs.

Place cheese sticks in single layer on foil-lined shallow baking pan sprayed with no stick cooking spray.
Bake 5 minutes or until cheese is softened but not melted. Serve with warmed marinara sauce.

MOTHER'S BROCCOLI CHEESE SOUP

MAKES APPROXIMATELY 12 SERVINGS

This collaboration of broccoli, cheese, and breast milk is one for the ages.

YOU WILL NEED :

1 cup of Mother's sweet breast milk

1 cup of whole milk (from the cow)

4 cans of chicken broth (14.5 ounces each)

1 cup of water (room temperature)

⅔ cup of cornstarch

1 whole yellow onion (chopped)

1 package of frozen chopped broccoli (chopped)

16 ounces of Velveeta cheese (cubed)

1 teaspoon salt

1 teaspoon garlic powder

4 ounces butter (unsalted)

DIRECTIONS:

Melt butter over medium heat in a large stockpot. Add chopped onion and cook in butter until onion becomes soft. Stir in broccoli and chicken broth. Cover pot and simmer for approximately 12 minutes until broccoli is tender.

Add Velveeta cheese cubes and stir continuously until cheese is melted. Reduce heat to low and mix in breast milk, cow's milk, salt, and garlic powder.

In a separate bowl, mix cornstarch into water until dissolved. Add cornstarch mixture into soup stirring continuously. Cook soup until thick, stirring frequently. Once soup has reached desired thickness, spoon into bowls or bread bowls and serve. Garnish with parsley if desired.

MOTHER'S ANGEL FOOD CAKE

MAKES APPROXIMATELY 8 SERVINGS

This recipe is so angelic, it tastes like it was delivered fresh from heaven.

YOU WILL NEED :

2 tablespoons of Mother's sweet breast milk

1 ¾ cups granulated sugar

1 ¼ cups of cake flour

1 ½ cups of egg whites

½ teaspoon pure vanilla extract

½ teaspoon almond extract

1 teaspoon cream of tartar

1 ¼ teaspoon salt

DIRECTIONS:

Beat egg whites until they stiffen, forming peaks. Then add breast milk, cream of tartar, pure vanilla extract, and almond extract. Lightly stir together.

In a medium bowl, sift together cake flour, granulated sugar, and salt. Repeat the sifting process 4 times so dry ingredients are well mixed.

Combine wet ingredients with dry ingredients gently. Pour finished cake batter evenly into an non-greased cake pan. You can use a 10-inch loaf pan or a round cake pan as desired.

Place pan in cold oven on center rack and turn oven temperature on to 325° F. Bake for approximately 1 hour until cake is golden brown.

Remove from oven and invert cake allowing it to cool in pan. Once cake is thoroughly cooled, remove from pan and serve.

MOTHER'S STRAWBERRY
BANANA SMOOTHIE

MAKES APPROXIMATELY 2 SERVINGS

Easy to prepare, and goes down just as easy.

YOU WILL NEED :

½ cup of Mother's sweet breast milk

¼ cup of whole milk (from the cow)

1 ¼ cups of fresh strawberries

2 whole bananas (frozen)

½ cup of ice cubes

1 teaspoon granulated sugar

Whipped topping (optional)

DIRECTIONS:

Thoroughly wash strawberries and chop into pieces.
Place chopped strawberries into a blender.

Carefully slice frozen bananas and place in blender with
strawberries. Add breast milk, cow's milk, sugar, and ice cubes.
Mix ingredients on low until well blended.

Pour blended mixture into two tall glasses and serve. Top
each glass with whipped topping if desired.

MOTHER'S RICH & SWEET CHOCOLATE CAKE

MAKES APPROXIMATELY 6 SERVINGS

Who ever said you can't have your cake and eat it too?

YOU WILL NEED :

¼ cup Mother's sweet breast milk

¾ cup of water

2 cups granulated sugar

2 cups of all-purpose flour

2 large eggs (lightly beaten)

⅓ cup of unsalted butter

1 teaspoon pure vanilla extract

5 ounces unsweetened chocolate chips

2 teaspoons baking powder

2 teaspoons baking soda

1 teaspoon salt

3 tablespoons all-purpose flour (for cake pans)

1 store-bought container of chocolate frosting (12 ounces)

DIRECTIONS:

Preheat oven to 350° F. Butter and flour two 9-inch round cake pans and set aside.

In a medium bowl, sift together flour, baking soda, baking powder, and salt. Set aside.

In a medium saucepan, combine the water and granulated sugar and bring to a boil over high heat. Keep stirring until sugar dissolves. Once sugar has dissolved, remove from heat and pour sugar water into a large mixing bowl. Add breast milk, chocolate chips, and butter. Sir mixture occasionally until melted. Add vanilla extract and stir slowly, allowing mixture to cool slightly. Use an electric mixer to blend in the beaten eggs at medium speed until combined. Now add all of the dry ingredients at once and beat at medium speed until smooth.

Divide the finished cake batter evenly into the two prepared cake pans. Place both cake pans on center rack in oven and bake for 25 to 30 minutes. Check if cake is done by inserting a toothpick in the center of the cake and removing it (toothpick should come out clean). Remove both cakes from oven and allow them to cool in pans for about 30 minutes. Now remove both cakes from pans by inverting and allow cakes to finish cooling on a rack for about 15 minutes.

On a serving platter, place one of the cakes right-side-up and spread ⅓ of the chocolate frosting evenly over the top using a spatula. Place the second cake on top and use the remainder of the chocolate frosting to cover the top and sides evenly. The finished cake is now ready to be cut into slices and served.

MOTHER'S MILKY COCONUT CREAM PIE

MAKES APPROXIMATELY 8 SERVINGS

A cream pie can come in many forms, but this coconut version is our favorite.

YOU WILL NEED :

1 cup of Mother's sweet breast milk

1 pre-made pie crust

10 oz of coconut milk

2 cups of shredded or flaked toasted coconut

1 ½ teaspoons vanilla

¾ cup of sugar

¼ teaspoon of salt

5 egg yolks

¼ cup of cornstarch

½ teaspoon of coconut extract

1 tablespoon of butter

16 oz whipped cream

DIRECTIONS:

Preheat oven to 350° F.

Brush small amount of coconut milk onto the pre-made pie crust and then sprinkle ½ cup of the toasted coconut onto the dough, press into the dough just enough to make it stick. Bake 8-10 minutes. Set aside to cool.

Heat in a saucepan the remaining coconut milk, Mama's sweet breast milk, vanilla, ¾ cup of sugar, and the salt on medium to high heat, stir occasionally, until it starts to simmer.

In a separate bowl, whisk the egg yolks, the remaining sugar and the cornstarch until even. Once even, add the mixture to the saucepan.

Heat the mixture to a simmer over medium to high heat, constantly mixing with the whisk 5-7 minutes or until the mixture is thickened.

Remove from the heat and beat in the coconut extract and butter. Pour the mixture into the crust, wrap in plastic wrap, and place in the refrigerator for at least 1 hour.

Before serving, spread the whipped cream over the pie until the cooled filling is covered. Sprinkle the rest of the toasted coconut flakes on top of the whipped cream as desired.

VANILLA PUDDING CAKE

MAKES APPROXIMATELY 8 SERVINGS

Grandma's comfort food at its finest.

YOU WILL NEED :

½ cup of Mother's sweet breast milk

2 tablespoons of butter

1 cup of sugar

2 teaspoons vanilla

⅔ cup of flour

½ cup of unsweetened cocoa

1 teaspoon of baking powder

1 teaspoon of salt

½ cup of cooking oats

1 ½ cups of boiling water

DIRECTIONS:

In a bowl combine the butter, ½ cup of sugar, the vanilla, flour, ¼ cup cocoa, the baking powder, and ½ teaspoon of salt. Add Mama's sweet breast milk to the mixture stir, add the oats while stirring.

In a cake pan combine the remaining sugar, remaining cocoa, remaining salt, and the boiling water, then add the previous mixture to the cake pan.

Bake in oven at 350° F for 45 to 60 minutes.

Best served warm.

MOTHER'S RICE KRISP

MAKES APPROXIMATELY 8 SERVINGS

Fun to make with the whole family, this gooey recipe is definitely finger-licking good.

YOU WILL NEED :

3 tablespoons of butter

¼ cup of Mother's sweet breast milk

4 cups of miniature marshmallows

6 cups of Rice Krispies® cereal

DIRECTIONS:

In a large pan, melt the butter over low heat. Add marshmallows and Mama's sweet breast milk. Stir until the marshmallows are completely melted.

Add the cereal and stir until uniform with spatula. Spread the mixture no more than 2 inches thick in a baking pan that has been sprayed with cooking spray. Let cool and cut into desired size squares.

Thank You

The Mothers Milk Cookbook would not be possible if it wasn't for our successful Kickstarter campaign. Thank you to the over one hundred supporters who pledged funds that went directly to the production of this book (these models weren't cheap). With the help of our backers, we were able to achieve our goal of providing the first cookbook of its kind, and making these amazing Mother's Milk recipes available for all to enjoy! We would not have been able to provide this quality product if not for your generosity. The following pages highlight some of our Kickstarter backers.

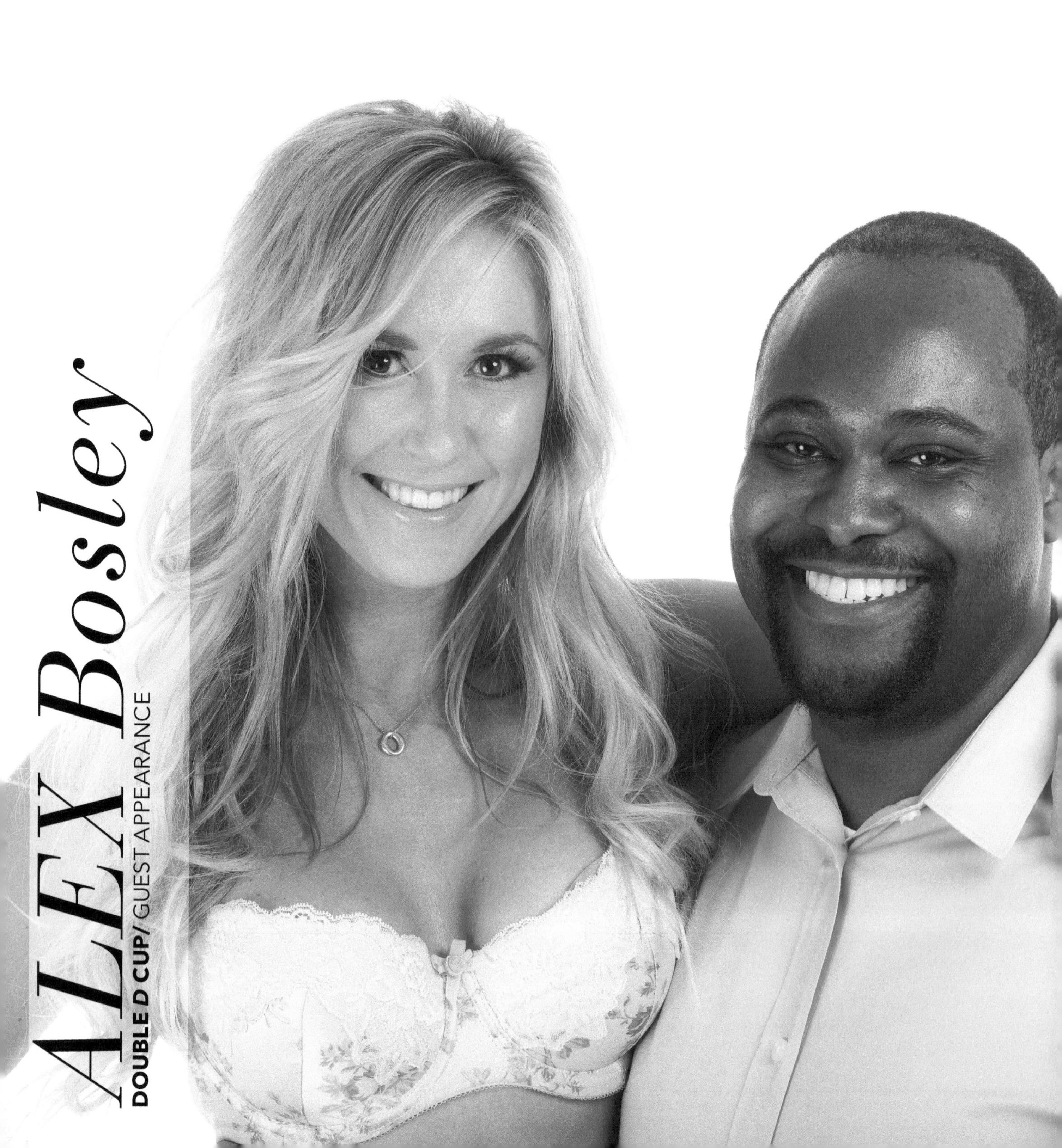
ALEX Bosley
DOUBLE D CUP/ GUEST APPEARANCE

TIMOTHY *Galindo*

DOUBLE D CUP/ GUEST APPEARANCE

DOUBLE D CUP / GUEST APPEARANCE

THANK YOU

BRYAN
Yee

&

KINJAL
Desai

DOUBLE *D* CUP

THANK YOU

SHAAN Mehta

JAMES Edleman

JONATHAN Pedersen

FRIENDS of PURPOSE, LLC

RYAN Nunokawa

MARK Hershey

TYLER Mahon

ARSEN karapogosian

THANK YOU

D CUP

ROBERT Cosci

MICHAEL *"Waffles"* Nguyen

NIKKI Jolee

PAOLO Tang

BENJAMIN Benditson

MICHAEL Lopez

ELY S. Tirao

MAO

LOGAN Ketchum

ANDREW Kelso

PAUL

ED

MARC EWING

VINCENT Yu

JESSICA Buzel

MICHAEL Pelikan

GORGE Lozano

TRICIA Kawasaki

THOMAS Rippy

Mark Rodriguez HYPHY

RUDI Lux

C CUP

THANK YOU

ALEXIS Richter

STEVEN Ross

NICHOLAS O'Neal

AIKAGI000

SHERELLE Johnson

JAVIER AcuÃ±a

biologist_jerry

JONATHAN Wirth

ELIGOR

DANIEL Jodin

B CUP

THANK YOU

- BRAD Zamora
- TONY Palka
- JMMul
- HIROKAZU Sakamoto
- KAITLIN Black
- JOSEPH Manning
- ALISHA Biggs
- RUSSELL Ketchum
- DANIEL Zapien
- ERIC Bardwell
- ERIC Bottomley
- MAXIMILIAN Merimee
- ANGEL Gonzalez
- JASON V. Holmes
- ROSALBA Jasso
- BRIAN V. Durkin
- ADAM Tomalas
- RACHEL Reynolds
- JON Legarte

A CUP

THANK YOU

GARRETT Liebman
DUSTIN Downing
KURT Ketchum
AARON
CHRISTOPHER Turoci
GAVIN Ketchum
DIEGO De Farias Diehl
BEN Hall
JONATHON Powell
ANTHONY V. Attalla
MARVIN Sanchez
WEI Chen
JESUS Calderon Jr.
MATT Lewis
DAVID Allison
ASIM Khurshid
CHRISTIAN Wheel
ROBERT E. Churney
DIAMOND Lane LTD

CPSIA information can be obtained
at www.ICGtesting.com
Printed in the USA
BVHW02n0853131018
529862BV00001B/1/P